Portraits of Paris

FROM THE LOUVRE TO THE EIFFEL TOWER

A TRAVEL PHOTO ART BOOK

LAINE CUNNINGHAM

Portraits of Paris

From the Louvre to the Eiffel Tower

A Travel Photo Art Book

Published by Sun Dogs Creations
Changing the World One Book at a Time
Print ISBN: 9781946732842

Cover Design by Angel Leya

Copyright © 2018 Laine Cunningham

All rights reserved. No part of this book may be reproduced in any form or by any means, electronic, mechanical, digital, photocopying or recording, except for the inclusion in a review, without permission in writing from the publisher.

THE TRAVEL PHOTO ART SERIES

Bikes of Berlin

Necropolises of New Orleans I & II

Ruins of Rome I & II

Ancients of Assisi I & II

Panoramas of Portugal

Nuances of New York

Glimpses of Germany

Impressions of Italy

Altitudes of the Alps

Coast of California

Utopia of the Unicorn

Knights Through the Ages

Flourishes of France

DRAGON LOCH

COMPASS ROSE

CAIRO

MEADOW FLOWERS

RUFFLED

RESPITE

MOSS

BEADED

BUTTONS

CONCORDE

HEAR NO EVIL

SAPLINGS

SHELTER FROM THE STORM

BIRDS ON A WIRE

SPIRE GRIN

WALK ON WATER

SPHINX

PRONOUNCEMENT

JUNKS

CINEMATIC

MIRRORED

ROYAL COURT

WALK IN THE VALLEY

VISITING FRIENDS

MINIATURE VATICAN

BOOKS RULE

CHATEAU

SLEEPING ELEPHANT

HIDEAWAY

SPROUTS

About the Author

Laine Cunningham's books take readers around the world. *The Family Made of Dust* is set in the Australian Outback, while *Reparation* is a novel of the American Great Plains. Her women's travel adventure memoir *Woman Alone: A Six-Month Journey Through the Australian Outback* appeals to fans of *Wild* and *Eat Pray Love*.

Fiction

The Family Made of Dust

Beloved

Reparation

Nonfiction

Woman Alone

On the Wallaby Track: Australian Words and Phrases

Seven Sisters: Messages from Aboriginal Australia

Writing While Female or Black or Gay

The Zen of Travel
The Zen of Gardening
Zen in the Stable
The Zen of Chocolate
The Zen of Dogs

The Wisdom of Puppies
The Wisdom of Babies
The Wisdom of Weddings

Bikes of Berlin
Necropolises of New Orleans I & II
Ruins of Rome I & II
Ancients of Assisi I & II
Panoramas of Portugal
Nuances of New York
Glimpses of Germany
Impressions of Italy
Altitudes of the Alps
Knights Through the Ages
Coast of California
Utopia of the Unicorn
Portraits of Paris
Flourishes of France

www.ingramcontent.com/pod-product-compliance
Lightning Source LLC
Chambersburg PA
CBHW041322110526
44591CB00021B/2874